SUPER SIMPLE
SCANDINAVIAN ART

FUN AND EASY ART FROM AROUND THE WORLD

ALEX KUSKOWSKI

Super Sandcastle

An Imprint of Abdo Publishing
www.abdopublishing.com

Consulting Editor, Diane Craig,
M.A./Reading Specialist

VISIT US AT WWW.ABDOPUBLISHING.COM

Published by Abdo Publishing, a division of ABDO, PO Box 398166, Minneapolis, Minnesota 55439. Copyright © 2015 by Abdo Consulting Group, Inc. International copyrights reserved in all countries. No part of this book may be reproduced in any form without written permission from the publisher. Super SandCastle™ is a trademark and logo of Abdo Publishing.

Printed in the United States of America, North Mankato, Minnesota
062014
092014

THIS BOOK CONTAINS RECYCLED MATERIALS

Editor: Liz Salzmann
Content Developer: Nancy Tuminelly
Cover and Interior Design and Production: Mighty Media, Inc.
Photo Credits: Jen Schoeller, Shutterstock

The following manufacturers/names appearing in this book are trademarks: Elmer's® Glue-All™, Sharpie®, Kemps®, Odense, Roundy's®

Library of Congress Cataloging-in-Publication Data
Kuskowski, Alex., author.
  Super simple Scandinavian art : fun and easy art from around the world / Alex Kuskowski ; consulting editor, Diane Craig, M.A., reading specialist.
    pages cm. -- (Super simple cultural art)
  Audience: Ages 5-10.
  ISBN 978-1-62403-283-7
1. Handicraft--Juvenile literature. 2. Scandinavia--Civilization--Miscellanea--Juvenile literature. I. Craig, Diane, editor. II. Title. III. Series: Super simple cultural art.
  TT160.K8744 2015
  745.50948--dc23
                        2013043459

Super SandCastle™ books are created by a team of professional educators, reading specialists, and content developers around five essential components—phonemic awareness, phonics, vocabulary, text comprehension, and fluency—to assist young readers as they develop reading skills and strategies and increase their general knowledge. All books are written, reviewed, and leveled for guided reading, early reading intervention, and Accelerated Reader® programs for use in shared, guided, and independent reading and writing activities to support a balanced approach to literacy instruction.

TO ADULT HELPERS

Children can have a lot of fun learning about different cultures through arts and crafts. Be sure to supervise them as they work on the projects in this book. Let the kids do as much as possible on their own. But be ready to step in and help if necessary. Also, kids may be using glue, paint, markers, and clay. Make sure they protect their clothes and work surfaces.

TABLE OF CONTENTS

DANISH HEARTS

In Denmark, children fold paper into heart-shaped baskets. They hang them on their Christmas trees!

COOL CULTURE

Get ready to go on a **cultural** art adventure! All around the world, people make art. They use art to show different **traditions** and ideas. Learning about different cultures with art can be a lot of fun.

Scandinavia is a region of Europe. Scandinavia usually means the countries of Norway, Sweden, and Denmark. Iceland and Finland are sometimes included in Scandinavia.

Learn more about Scandinavian countries! Try some of the art projects in this book. Get creative with culture using art.

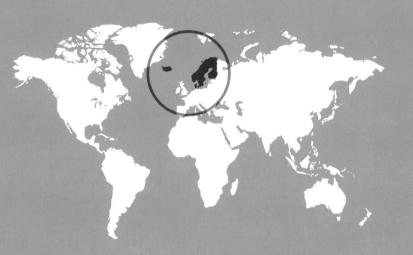

BEFORE YOU START

Remember to treat other people and **cultures** with respect. Respect their art, **jewelry**, and clothes too. These things can have special meaning to people.

There are a few rules for doing art projects:

▶ **PERMISSION**
Make sure to get **permission** to do a project. You might want to use things you find around the house. Ask first!

▶ **SAFETY**
Get help from an adult when using something hot or sharp. Never use a stove or oven by yourself.

ART IN SCANDINAVIAN CULTURE

People in Scandinavia create many beautiful things. Some are for everyday use. Others are for special occasions. The **designs** in Scandinavian art often have special meanings.

 Vikings lived in Scandinavia more than 1,000 years ago. They sailed all over the world.

 A Paskris is a tree decorated with feathers. Making them is a Swedish springtime **tradition**.

 Dala horses have been carved in Sweden for nearly 400 years.

 Lapland is an area in Northern Sweden and Finland. The Sami people are native to this area.

 At Christmas, Scandinavians often serve **porridge** with an almond hidden in it. Whoever gets the almond wins a lucky marzipan pig.

 Every year, straw ornaments decorate Christmas trees all over Scandinavia.

WHAT YOU NEED

acrylic paint, paint brush, & foam brush

bowl

branches

colored feathers

colored paper

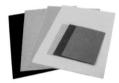
craft foam

craft glue

dinner knife

drinking straws

felt

glass rocks

glass vase

hole punch

masking tape

measuring cup

newspaper

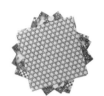

patterned paper

pencil & marker

pint-size milk carton

red food coloring

ribbon

rubber eraser

ruler

scissors

small wooden block

string

toothpicks

white marzipan

wooden skewers

yarn

PERFECT PAPER HEARTS

Take this fun bag with you wherever you go!

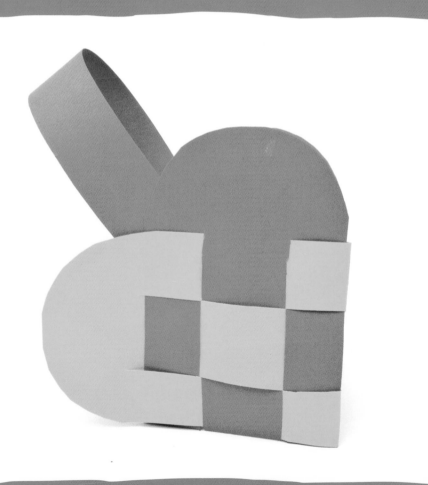

WHAT YOU NEED

red and yellow paper

scissors

ruler

pencil

craft glue

DIRECTIONS

1. Cut a piece of red paper 3 inches (7.6 cm) by 9 inches (23 cm). Fold it in half.

2. Round off the corners opposite the fold.

3. Cut two slits starting at the fold. Make the slits 3 inches (7.6 cm) long. Space the slits evenly.

4. Repeat steps 1 through 3 with the yellow paper.

PROJECT CONTINUES ON THE NEXT PAGE

DIRECTIONS (CONTINUED)

(5) Label the three strips on the red paper A, B, and C. Label the three strips on the yellow paper 1, 2, and 3. Use pencil so you can erase the labels later.

(6) Stick strip C through strip 1. Stick strip 1 through strip B. Stick strip A through strip 1.

(7) Stick strip 2 through strip C. Stick strip B through strip 2. Stick strip 2 through strip A.

DIRECTIONS (CONTINUED)

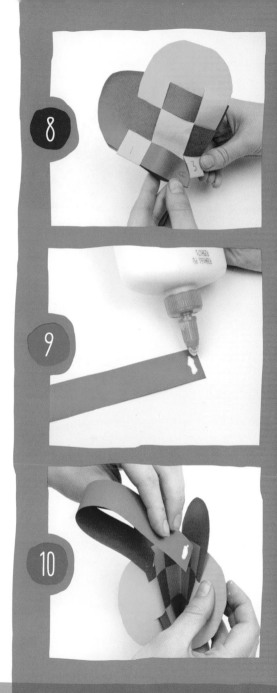

8. Stick strip C through strip 3. Stick strip 3 through strip B. Stick strip A through strip 3.

9. Cut a strip of paper 8 inches (20.3 cm) by 1 inch (2.5 cm). Put glue on one end.

10. Press the end of the strip to the inside of the basket. Put glue on the other end of the strip. Press it to the other side of the basket. Let the glue dry.

11. Erase any visible pencil marks.

DALA HORSE STAMP

Decorate your home with a true Scandinavian symbol!

WHAT YOU NEED

red craft foam

marker

scissors

craft glue

small wooden block

rubber erasers

red, yellow, and blue acrylic paint

paintbrush

plain paper

DIRECTIONS

① Draw a horse on red craft foam. Draw a saddle and mane on the horse. Cut out the horse. Cut out the saddle and mane.

2 Glue the foam horse to the wooden block. Let the glue dry.

③ Glue the saddle to an eraser. Glue the mane to an eraser. Let the glue dry.

④ Paint the horse red. Turn the wooden block over. Press it onto a piece of paper. Lift up the stamp. Let the paint dry.

⑤ Paint the saddle blue. Press it to the paper in the saddle shape on the horse. Paint the mane yellow. Stamp it on the paper in the mane shape.

QUICK TIP: Wash the stamps when you are done. You can reuse them.

STRAW ORNAMENT

Make an ornament to hang anywhere!

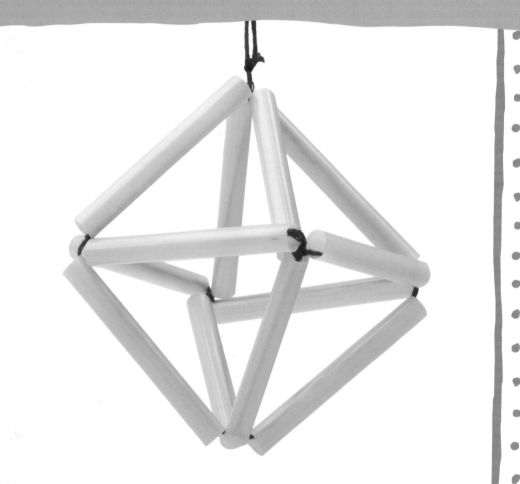

WHAT YOU NEED

yellow drinking straws

ruler

scissors

red string

craft glue

book

pushpin

DIRECTIONS

1. Cut the straws into 12 pieces, 2 inches (5 cm) long. Cut a piece of string 3 feet (1 m) long.

2. Put four straws on the string. Push the straws to one end of the string. Form the straws into a diamond. Tie the ends of the string together.

3. Cut off the shorter end of the string.

PROJECT CONTINUES ON THE NEXT PAGE

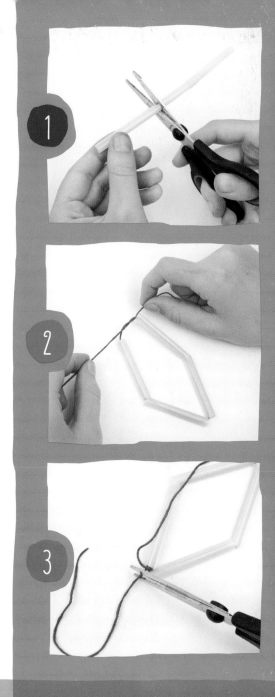

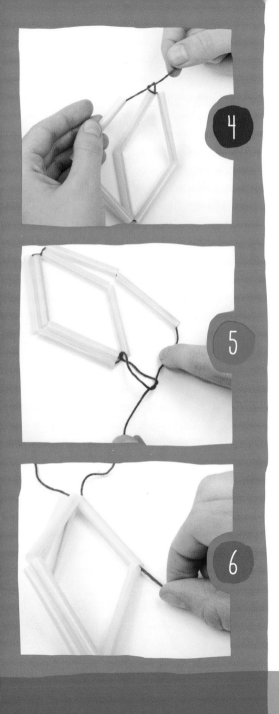

DIRECTIONS (CONTINUED)

4 Put two straws on the string. Tie the string between the straws at the opposite end of the diamond.

5 Put two more straws on the string. Tie the string between the straws at the opposite end of the diamond.

6 Thread the string back through one of the straws near the last knot you tied.

DIRECTIONS (CONTINUED)

7. Add one straw. Tie the string between the nearest two straws.

8. Add another straw. Tie the string between the next two straws. Add the last two straws the same way.

9. Tie the end of the string to the string near the straws. This makes a **loop** for hanging the ornament.

LAPLAND HEADBAND

Make a fun headband that will keep you warm!

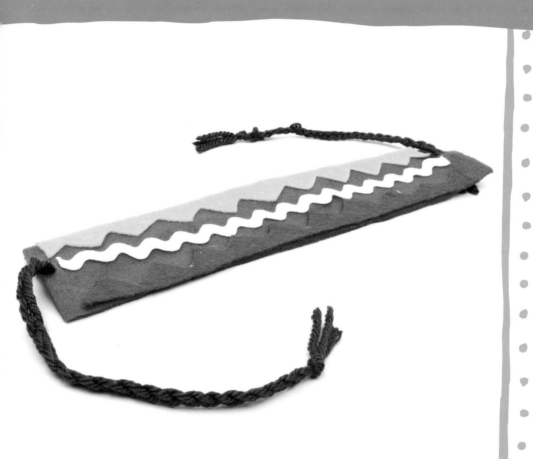

WHAT YOU NEED

red, yellow, and green felt

scissors

ruler

craft glue

zigzag ribbon

hole punch

yarn

Directions

1. Cut a piece of red felt 10 inches (25.5 cm) by 2 inches (5 cm). Cut pieces of yellow and green felt 9 inches (23 cm) by 1 inch (2.5 cm). Cut the yellow and green pieces in half **lengthwise**. Cut them in a zigzag pattern.

2. Glue a yellow piece along one side of the red felt. Glue a green piece along the other side. Glue a piece of zigzag ribbon down the middle. Let the glue dry.

3. Punch a hole in one end of the felt. Cut three pieces of yarn 12 inches (30.5 cm) long. Stick them all through the hole. Tie the ends together in a large knot. Pull the knot against the back of the felt. Braid the yarn.

4. Tie a knot at the end of the braid.

5. Repeat steps 3 and 4 to **attach** a braid to the other end of the band.

FUN FEATHERED TREE

Make this tree to get into the springtime spirit!

WHAT YOU NEED

newspaper

branches

white acrylic paint

foam brush

colored feathers

scissors

white string

glass vase

glass rocks

pencil

ruler

colored paper

patterned paper

craft glue

ribbon

hole punch

DIRECTIONS

1. Cover your work area with newspaper. Paint the branches white. Let the paint dry.

2. Place a feather near the end of a branch. Wrap a piece of string around the feather and the branch. Wrap it a few times and then tie it in a knot.

3. Repeat step 2 to add more feathers to the branches.

4. Fill the vase halfway with glass rocks. Add the feathered branches.

PROJECT CONTINUES ON THE NEXT PAGE

DIRECTIONS (CONTINUED)

5. Draw an egg shape 3 inches (7.6 cm) long on patterned paper. Draw a slightly larger egg shape on the colored paper.

6. Cut out the eggs.

7. Glue the smaller egg on top of the larger egg.

DIRECTIONS (CONTINUED)

8. Punch a hole at one end of the egg.

9. Cut a piece of ribbon 9 inches (23 cm) long. Thread the ribbon through the hole in the egg. Tie the ends of the ribbon together.

10. Repeat steps 5 through 9 to make more paper eggs. Hang the eggs on the branches.

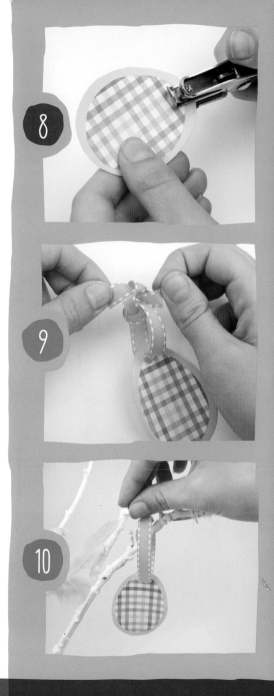

VIKING SAILING SHIP

Sail the seas with the Scandinavians!

2 pint-size milk cartons

ruler

marker

scissors

craft glue

brown paper

marker

newspaper

acrylic paint

foam brush

wooden skewer

masking tape

plain paper

DIRECTIONS

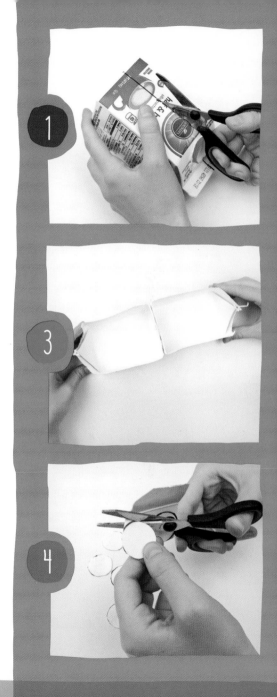

1. Lay a carton down with the front facing up. Measure 1 inch (2.5 cm) in from one side. Draw a line around the carton. Cut along the line.

2. Repeat step 1 with the other carton.

3. Glue the bottoms of the smaller carton pieces together. Let the glue dry.

4. Cut six 1-inch (2.5 cm) circles out of the larger carton pieces.

PROJECT CONTINUES ON THE NEXT PAGE

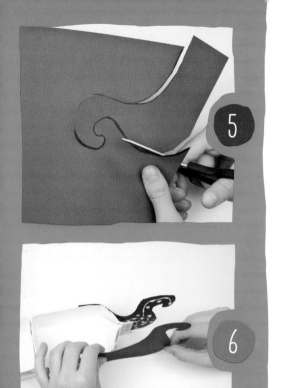

(5) Draw a curved boat **prow** on brown paper. The end opposite the prow should be 1 inch (2.5 cm) wide and 3 inches (7.6 cm) long. Cut it out. Trace the shape three times. Cut out the shapes.

(6) Match two prows together. Glue the other ends to either side of a carton. Glue the prows together. Glue the remaining prows to the other carton the same way. Let the glue dry.

(7) Cover your work area with newspaper. Paint the boat brown. Let the paint dry. Add another coat of paint. Paint the skewer brown. Let it dry.

DIRECTIONS (CONTINUED)

8. Tape the skewer to the middle of the boat.

9. Paint the circles teal and red. Let the paint dry. Glue three of the circles to each side of the boat.

10. Paint red stripes across a sheet of paper. Let the paint dry. Cut the paper to 9 inches (23 cm) by 6 inches (15 cm).

11. Push one side of the paper onto the skewer. Pull it down a few inches. Push the opposite side of the paper onto the skewer.

MARZIPAN PIG TREAT

Make your own good luck charm!

WHAT YOU NEED

white marzipan

measuring cup

bowl

red food coloring

dinner knife

toothpick

DIRECTIONS

1. Put ¼ cup marzipan in a bowl. Add two drops of food coloring. Mix them together with your hands.

2. Roll a tube 4 inches (10 cm) long and ¾ inch (2 cm) wide. Cut it into 1 inch (2.5 cm) pieces. These are the pig's legs. Stand the legs together side by side.

3. Roll a ball about 2 inches (5 cm) wide. Set it on top of the legs. Press down gently.

4. Make a small, flat disk for the nose. Press it to the body. Make two small triangles for ears. Press them to the top of the body.

5. Use the toothpick to poke two holes in the nose. Poke two holes for the eyes.

GLOSSARY

attach – to join or connect.

culture – the ideas, art, and other products of a particular group of people.

design – a decorative pattern or arrangement.

jewelry – pretty things, such as rings and necklaces, that you wear for decoration.

lengthwise – in the direction of the longest side.

loop – a circle made by a rope, string, or wire.

permission – when a person in charge says it's okay to do something.

porridge – a soft food, such as oatmeal, made by boiling grain in milk or water.

prow – the front of a boat or ship.

tradition – a belief or practice passed through a family or group of people.